Through Heaven's Eyes

Karla Fletcher

Through Heaven's Eyes © 2022

Karla fletcher

Presentation by *BookLeaf Publishing*

Web: www.bookleafpub.com

E-mail: info@bookleafpub.com

ISBN: 978-93-5744-477-4

First edition 2022

This book is dedicated to Marilyn "Boogie" Fletcher who gave me the wings to soar with eagles, the confidence to have my own voice and the strength to use that voice as a means to advocate for myself as well as others.

ACKNOWLEDGEMENT

Thank you to BookLeaf Publishing for this chance to be seen and heard.

Today's The Day

Today's the day I brought a cake, I counted
the candles over and over to make sure I got it
right.
I got you balloons and I made your favorite
dinner.
Now all I can do is wait for you to arrive home.
Yet the minutes seem to turn to hours
and now there is ice cream all over the floor.
Yet I am sitting here staring at the door.
Then it hits me like a ton of bricks.
You're not coming the drive is just too
far I'm sure you would still visit it just won't be
by car.
For the time it would take we can't count in
days.
But instead, I count it in heartbeats and
memories we made.
Heaven is just simply too far away.
They don't allow me to call collect and there are
no visiting hours no not today.
Though it hurt so much to lose you.
I couldn't possibly make you stay.
I know there is no pain up there.
So watch me my angel and see all
the things I come through.

My trials and tribulations aren't as hard so thank
you.
Thank you for teaching me how to be strong
Thank you for teaching me right from wrong.
But mommy dearest who I love so much you
forgot to teach me one thing even though
all these seem like enough – How to live in a
world without you. Happy birthday in heaven
a first I wish never had to come.
Though I thank
God your pain is over
I just wish you weren't gone.

But Why Now

This should be a happy time
This moment should be filled with happy tears
but instead it's filled with pain and regret
the pain of a thousand years could not
compare to what I feel on this day
it's three days till my special day
the day I have waited for all my life
the day you and dad probably thought would
never come
it's my wedding day and now
there is an empty place at the table
and an empty space within my heart
because we are just so far apart
why did you have to go so soon
why did you have to leave me without saying
goodbye
what I would do for more time
just one more day
but why now do all these
feelings have to come back
but why now do all these memories
have to flood my heart like
Moses parting the sea
I feel my heart was torn in half
the day your heart stopped beating
mine stopped too

because I do not know how to live on
this earth without you

Not Forgotten

I do not hear it as much as I used to
I miss it more than I would like to admit
I know I hated it before but now I long for it
forever more
I miss your cooking I miss your scent
I miss how we would argue I miss how I swore
I knew it all how I knew better than you
and how I was just too grown now
but I miss it so much and I wish someone would
say it
just one last time
I wish I could pull up your picture or hear your
voice
and someone say those words I hated for all
those years
You look just like your mother.
It seems like some have forgotten
But no not I
I have never forgotten your face
your voice
and your grace
you will forever have a place
within my heart

25 Years

Twenty-five years of love
Of I'm proud of you
Twenty-five years of advice
Twenty-five years were not enough
Not enough time to say I love you
Not enough time to prepare me for this
Not enough time to show you
I would be ok
Not enough time
Not enough time to say thank you
For staying up to 1 AM
When I worked late at night
In a blink of an eye, you were gone
And I had to grow up right then and there
Now I just have the memories of your voice
And wishing you were there
Remember when you taught me to tie my shoes
Remember when you held my hand as I learned
to walk
Twenty-five years seemed like it flew by
And as much as I would argue that I was not a
child
I was your baby girl
For twenty-five years, I lived the blessed life
And though I know all wounds will heal with
time

I would climb every mountain for twenty-five
more with you
I wasn't ready to let go
I lost a parent but gained an Angel
So now there is no way I can fail

An Unfair Day

For a day that seems unfair
For a hero who isn't there
For the empty chair
That was once filled
For a house that was once filled with memories
For when those memories now bring the hardest
of tears cried
For the hardest goodbye of your life
When words cut deeper than a knife
Remember me for I am there
I'm the sun on your skin
The sound of the air
I am still there with you
There for you
For the days that are long
Look for me
See the signs
They are still there
I cared then
And continue to care now
You may think me gone
But it's far from the truth
Because I live on through
You

Left Unsaid

So many words left unsaid
so many feelings that knock into me
like the Titanic, I am going down
sinking into the emotions of hate
and anger the tears hit like
bullets in the midst of a war
but this one seems like it will never be won
so many things I want to tell you
but I don't know how
how do I reach you
when you are so far away
even a glimpse of heaven
would help me make it
through another day without you
I want to tell you about my wedding
I want to tell you about my dream job
I want to tell you about all the bad
hair cuts in between
I want to tell you about how
I couldn't get into my wedding dress
these are the things left unsaid
because you aren't near
these are the things that keep me
up at night
it's just not right
it's just not fair

how can God take someone from me
who is just so dear

Momma Hold My Hand

Momma
please hold my hand
hold me like you used to do
when I was young and needed you
I still need you
while I can stand on my own two feet
I am unstable
without you there to catch me
if I fall
The day you left me
I fell to the ground in prayer
I begged God
I begged God to just
leave you there
I needed you
Couldn't you hear me
I surely screamed it loud enough
How could you do this to me
I screamed it loud enough
Please don't go
But still, you went

Never Enough

We had twenty-eight amazing years
yet it was not enough
we had 14716800 minutes together
and yet in one single second all those
wonderful minutes
all those wonderful memories
all those wonderful times
seem to disappear from my mind
like amnesia, I can't remember anything
before those words I am sorry
they pronounced you so fast
it seems like without a care
they walked away
and I cried
I cried for the memories
I cried for the moments
I would have without you
The day would feel so long now
The nights would last forever
The time was just never enough

Wedding Day Vibes

It's my special day
the ones that probably seemed like a lifetime
away
It's my wedding day
wedding bells will be ringing
the dress will be white
I'll have something new
I'll have something old
and I'll be the something blue
because I am nothing without you
Where are you on this special day
You won't even get to try the cake
The life my husband and I shall make
The vibes are just not the same
without you there to
help me get dressed
to give me away
it's my wedding day
it's just not the same

Does

Does it tear you apart
when the beating of a hard-working heart
stops
does it bring you to your knees
when you are begging the lord
please
please
Does seeing the
deceased seem hard on the eyes
does it just make you want to cry
and just look to the lord and say why
Life just slipping away
there will not be any other days
Does this bring back all the silly wants
when now all you want is one more moment

One last hope

One last hope
Soul
I beg for forgiveness
to forever invade
silent, tortured
Maybe one day
things will be ok
but that day isn't today
because I can't stop the tears
that are coming
it's mourning the life
that I knew
May space and time
come upon us
torn, bleak, and anew like
a child,
and so I pray in
an instant, a flash
A troubled heart
could find rest
forever invading the feelings of fear
there is only an illusion
torn, soulless for a minute
a second, a day
somehow once again I shall be ok

Goodbye Mom

They say all good things must end
connected for always, you said
as I clasp my hands and pray
your feelings washed away by life's constant toll
They say all good things must end
But you were the greatest
to me a hero
now an angel
all good things must come to an end
but why couldn't I just live in
the moment
and now the moment is gone
cause all good things must come to an end

Next Time

Tell ya, the next time around
I'll be here for you
And I'll be waiting by the door
So tell ya, the next time around
I'll be here for you and I will listen to you
And I'll be waiting by the door
I used to think there was something I could do
When I was down, lonely and alone just missing
you
I used to think that I had found a way
to show you
That my loneliness was just a sign
Of weakness, I'm telling you
That maybe I can be trusted
I'm standing here and it's you mommy that I
need
And there's nothin' that I could do cause you're
gone
And everything just seems so dark

Place Of Faith

I can't go on without you
I've found a place of faith
I got a long road to travel
I've had a few heavy drops of rain
And the water's still falling upon my feet
So much for simple things
And simple things are just things I'd do
In dark, we turn to prayer
And light our streets with
Hope for peace and justice
And if we make plans to leave this place
And find some other place to stay
There's a dark cloud hanging above me
I need you,
I need you,
I don't know where
I can be me where I can go where
this would not affect me
An invisible hand lifted me higher upon the sky
with the angels, I shall soar

You'll be on your way

You'll be on your way
You're always
On your way
And you'll know
You'll be on your way
up to Heaven where there is no pain
When you left and let go there was no shame
and yet we still speak your name
like you're still here with us
And it's not that easy sometimes
To be up at night and feel this tired
And crying in your sleep, oh
Tired of listening to your heart
Just a little bit moved
So you had to go somewhere
It's not that easy sometimes,
it's not that easy sometimes
Sometimes it's not that hard
It just feels like Hell every day
Like every fight is going into overtime
sometimes, it's not that easy
Sometimes it's not that hard, it's not that easy

I'll Be Fine

Somehow someway
I will be ok
I will be fine
it's just that
the pain hits me like a million
knives all at once
like falling down
in a blizzard
I'm covered in the coldness and the silence
that comes when you
have to let go of someone
who meant so much
the feelings that come
when you feel that time was not done
I'll be fine, this is not an SOS
I can find a way to be ok
even if it is just for one more day
one more minute, one more second
I can find a way to be ok, to find the peace
that I once knew
the peace I had before I lost you

One Last Time

I would love to hear it
just one last time
I would love to have someone
say it to me again like they
did when I was a kid
when I hated to hear it
When I argued with every breath
of my being
Now I miss those simple words
that seemed like sour grapes before
but now are sweeter than the
world's finest honey
just one more time
I would love to hear
you look just like
your mom

Till The End

Till the end, you held on
Till the end, you remained strong
cool and confident
even when the pain set in
Till the end, you remained
calm, cool and collected
Till the end, you held on to me
and to all of your friends
Till the end, I prayed
for a miracle
I prayed for the pain to end
I prayed that God would heal you
and he did
But in the process, he had to
take you to a new place
a place I cannot go
Till the end